Look Outside

Written by Cameron Macintosh

Look outside.

What can you see?

It is spring now.

I can see pink flowers
on the trees.

4

I can see children outside too.

It is summer now.

The leaves on the trees are green.

6

We can all go for a picnic outside.

It is autumn now.

The leaves are red and brown.

Anna is helping to clear up the leaves.

It is winter now.

I can see snow on the trees.

The snow is lots of fun!

Picture Glossary

 spring

 summer

 autumn

 winter